THE PERFECT PRICE

 THE PERFECT PRICE

THE PERFECT PRICE

THE PERFECT PRICE

 THE PERFECT PRICE

INDEX

Prices: all you need to know

Working with price-sensitive buyers

The "winning price"

Prices according to product type

Profit-enhancing pricing strategies

Skimming as a pricing strategy

Is the psychological price an effective strategy?

Market Penetration Prices

Promotional prices

Competitive price

Offer discounts as part of your pricing strategy

Alternative pricing strategies

Most attractive offers

Price based on value

How do you know if your price is right?

THE PERFECT PRICE

 THE PERFECT PRICE

Prices: all you need to know

If you are trying to sell something on the Internet, pricing your services/products would be the most important decision you will make. Since the Internet offers thousands of alternatives to customers, you must keep up with the competition. Prices will determine how long you can stay in the market.

You need to get a clear idea about prices. How far can you push it? How often do you need to review prices? A lot will depend on how you handle this stage of the business.

THE PERFECT PRICE

To start, you must identify a group of consumers and then estimate how much they would be willing to pay for your services or products.

But in addition to that, you must also make sure you get some benefit for yourself. And very often these two demands can be in conflict with each other. Different people use different techniques to price their products. Some of them have a scientific basis and others do not. Below is one such procedure that works with an understanding of the cost of production, customer expectations, and other actors in the field.

Cost is defined as the total sum of the expenses incurred in making a product. Expenses include the cost of raw materials, machinery, packaging, delivery, etc. Price is

THE PERFECT PRICE

the amount customers must pay per unit of their product/service.

In order for you to make a profit, the price must be more than the cost. Your prices should be consistently higher than cost if you plan to run your business for a long time, except in special cases. Sometimes you can lower prices, for example, to enter a market. Starting with lower prices than your competitors will make people notice you, and once you have a decent number of customers, you can gradually increase your prices!

How much customers pay for your services is directly proportional to how significant and valuable they believe your product is. Of course, you're marketing strategies and reputation in the marketplace will play an important role in this regard.

THE PERFECT PRICE

Between these two numbers, your cost and the price your customers are willing to pay for your product is your ideal price. If your price is a little lower than what your customers are willing to pay for your services, it will definitely work in your favor in the long run.

If your price is higher than what is fair in the eyes of the customer, you would end up losing your attractiveness and market and gradually lose your viability.

Working with price-sensitive buyers

The value of money in today's world is a harsh reality and that is why customers looking to buy for their needs have realized the effective factor when it comes to purchasing.

They are looking to get the most out of the least amount of money spent, which is why pricing your products correctly goes a long way to ensuring that you keep getting customers and making a profit. But that does not necessarily mean that you can only attract your customers by reducing prices, as this can often lead to losses.

But more than the price, it is the value of the product that determines its price in the eyes of the customer. You will never expect a high profile vehicle like a Mercedes to be priced like a Toyota, but they will expect to get the best deal from you when they look to buy a Toyota in the market.

Therefore, adding value to any product through good marketing, research and development is a sure way to ensure that your customer appreciates and accepts the price and value of the product. Therefore, it is a simple matter of changing the way the customer looks at a product.

The simplest and most efficient strategy for satisfying a price-sensitive buyer is to give

 THE PERFECT PRICE

them a vivid picture of the benefits this expense will bring them in the long run. Everyone likes to know that they spent good money on something that will last and bring more profit. So if you can convince the customer that buying something is not just about spending but investing in something that is worthwhile in the long run, they will definitely agree to spend the money.

By showing how the higher priced item will eventually cause minor problems and therefore save a lot of trouble and unnecessary expenses on services and repairs, you may be able to close the deal. Again, it is a matter of convincing your customers that they are doing the right thing by looking at the long-term benefits of the purchase.

 THE PERFECT PRICE

If you have a quality product and market it well, any sensible customer will come to you. Even if that means spending that extra money, customers want the best in the marketplace for them. Therefore, offering quality products never fails to attract customers for more.

Winning over price-sensitive buyers requires understanding that price is not the only component of your purchasing decisions. When you take the time to discover your customer's needs, you can present the full value of your service or customer. If you fail to uncover the full picture, you may find yourself in the position of answering price concerns and, in the long run, that will not help your business succeed.

Know your customers. Find out how their

minds work and what they want. This will go a long way in convincing and attracting them to buy the right, albeit expensive, product. If you don't understand that buying is not just about money but all the other things mentioned above, you may have to keep lowering prices to get customers and that will not be profitable for your business.

THE PERFECT PRICE

The "winning price"

Setting a price for your product or service, especially when you are trying to sell on the Internet, may be the most crucial business decision. Setting a price is not as simple as it might seem. If you're looking to make a profit, your price should be higher than your cost, but it should be lower than the "price the market can bear," the price your customers expect to pay for your service. You should keep this in mind when pricing your products.

There are elaborate pricing plans that you must understand and be able to work with. The pricing plan you want to work with will depend on your business model.

# THE PERFECT PRICE

So does the "Pricing to Penetrate" plan. This plan would work for you if your goal is to penetrate the target market quickly. To achieve this goal, you will need to price your product low.

But it is important to decide how low you can go without hitting rock bottom. You need to find out how low you can go without incurring debt and large losses. You should not have reservations about incurring initial losses if you will get long-term customers in return.

But how do you determine the lifetime value of any customer?

Insure your regular customers and make sure you take steps to get them to adhere to your

THE PERFECT PRICE

particular brand. Penetration pricing is useful if you are going to make a lasting impression. It can also be useful in circumstances where many new players are jumping into the market.

Your product should be the last "sticky product" that the customer can drop. Online brokers, for example, are much more convenient than once hooked, people don't even think about alternatives.

Another way to ensure that the customer comes back is to make an exceptional product. When selling books online, for example, a great book with a good price would guarantee instant popularity.

Amazon.com, for example, is the leading

THE PERFECT PRICE

player among online bookstores because of its highly subsidized rates. Although this marketing tactic could have cost them many thousands of dollars, they have managed to create a solid customer base that they can now trust.

Another viable example in real life is how companies that manufacture shaving machines come up against the idea that it would be much more profitable to resell razor blades than handles, and the rest, as they say, is history.

Prices according to product type

Finding the right price for your product is the key to success, both long and short term. The right price for your product would be between the cost and the price a customer is ready to pay for your services. The cost would include raw material expenses and other fixed and variable costs incurred in manufacturing. So much so, that it can also make your profits double or triple the current amount. Your products will technically fall into one of two categories:

Merchandise: there is a lot of competition in this field, because the products of the

different players on the field are the same, it's just the price they compete for. You must be very sharp and constantly alert. How competent and efficient you are are the only things that will make you stand out. A little bit of slack will mess things up again.

Proprietary Products: These are authentic products. Genuine and special in their own right. You compete with the other players in the market based on the special strengths of your services. If you are good enough and need it, you can set a price that guarantees you the best profit.

The market on the Internet is changing rapidly. To keep up, you may need to change your prices frequently, due to new competition and changes in demand, etc.

Then, there are certain products such as computer hardware that are commodities and proprietary. Computer systems are constantly being upgraded and become more sophisticated, and competition is fierce. It is a proprietary product in the sense that a Macintosh can still afford to be much more expensive than a normal Windows system because of the additional features it offers.

However, no matter what you do, you can't afford to put an incorrect price on your product because it can mean instant death in the marketplace.

Price wars today are part of every organization's daily existence. To survive, you must be constantly alert and deliver on

THE PERFECT PRICE

your promises. If even one competitor lowers his prices, everyone has to do the same. But if you are not going to do it, then you must have ample reason to stand firm. A solid customer base that stays with you no matter what can be a good reason.

Profit-enhancing pricing strategies

Pricing strategies are a sometimes overlooked part of the marketing mix. They can have a large impact on profits, so they should be given the same consideration as promotion and advertising strategies. A higher or lower price can dramatically change both gross margins and sales volume. This indirectly affects other expenses by reducing storage costs, for example, or by creating opportunities for volume discounts with suppliers.

Other factors also determine your optimal pricing strategy. Consider the five forces that

THE PERFECT PRICE

influence other business decisions: your competitors, your suppliers, the availability of substitute products, and your customers. Positioning how you want to be perceived by your target audience is also a consideration. Price a premium item too low, for example, and customers will not believe the quality is good enough. Conversely, put a too high selling price on the value lines and customers will buy lower priced items from the competition.

Some pricing strategies to consider are:

- Competitive Pricing

Keeping your prices in relation to your competitors is the best way to do business. Be aware of the price your competitor has next

THE PERFECT PRICE

to your products and then the prices similar or lower than yours.

- Cost plus surcharge

The full reverse of the above tactic mode, aims to set your prices according to your desire, according to the percentage of profit you want to keep and not the market. But just as this has the advantage of earning a lot through cheap pricing, this can also work negatively in certain circumstances. So think and decide wisely before you set the price.

- Loss leader

Another effective strategy to attract customers and increase sales considerably is

THE PERFECT PRICE

to sell relatively cheap items at a lower price to customers who have the potential to buy more expensive things. But this is a relatively temporary arrangement and can often be a gamble.

- Close

This is an interesting technique to try when you are cleaning your stock. This method involves selling your additional products at extremely cheap prices to avoid losses.

- Membership or trade discount

Get to know your customers. Make a short list of those who can benefit and give them special offers so that they end up being

enticed to buy more from you and keep coming back too. So reduce prices, offer discounts, do whatever it takes to get them to come back to your store.

- Packages and quantity discounts.

Simple plus one free also works very well. So, offer selected customers a substantial discount on bulk purchases, whether it's the same type, like 5 shirts, or similar or related items. And to avoid losses, place offers on old stock or form a new one with old ones to remove excess goods.

- Versioned

Putting different versions of the same basic

THE PERFECT PRICE

product and then offering lower prices for the more basic models is a good way to not only get rid of those models for average people. But you can also associate offers as a free service for a period with the higher priced ones to serve as an incentive for customers to buy more. So go ahead and use these tactics to get the level of profit you've always wanted.

Skimming as a pricing strategy

Of all the marketing strategies you will use in your business, the pricing strategy is one of the most important. In addition to choosing the right product, smart marketing and a solid sales plan, the right pricing strategy will determine your revenue and market share. Generally, your industry leaders use skimming the market as a pricing technique.

A computer manufacturer's strategy is to create a new laptop every 8 months or so. It reduces the price of older, unsold models (in their maturation stage) and keeps the price of new laptops (in their introduction stage)

 THE PERFECT PRICE

higher. New laptops will require a higher price based on their new features.

Therefore, the manufacturer is lowering the price (or lowering the market) at different stages: introduction, growth, maturity and decline. It gets the maximum benefit through the higher price each of these stages commands.

This strategy will work in a large market with enough buyers with a high demand for products or services and a company with a low cost structure. In the above example with the laptops, the demand is high; there are many recurring buyers with an industry that has a low cost structure that is technology enabled.

Now the challenge for the company comes from the fact that there are quite a few competitors in this market. If all of these competitors have a complete line of similar products, each with a variable life cycle, buyers will find it extremely difficult to judge the product in terms of its quality or service or value for money.

Faced with a flood of similar looking products, the buyer will choose a laptop with maximum features at the lowest price. And if your company is not the one with the lowest price, you may damage your brand reputation, as it will seem that you have been overpricing the products, eventually leading to a drop in sales.

Before choosing any pricing strategy, be sure to first study the market carefully. You should have a clear idea about the behavior of customers and how competitors will act or react. And this strategy should be continually tested as it is implemented to ensure that the factors that led to this strategy have not changed over time with changing market conditions.

Is the psychological price an effective strategy?

Price has an associated psychological meaning. Buyers believe that if a product has a high price, then it is more valuable. Although this belief is more psychological than reality-based, it makes the tangibles of pricing more effective than the product itself.

Interestingly, however, as the buyer begins to investigate the nature of the product more thoroughly, his decisions become more rational and the higher price ceases to be the measure of the product's value. A good example where the psychological prices are that buyers tend to be more inclined towards

THE PERFECT PRICE

prices that end in uneven numbers such as $9, $99 because they believe they are getting a better deal than if the prices ended in even numbers such as $20, $66 etc.

If the products being priced are in a "band" of prices like in online auctions or if they have a price in an odd range of $199.00, then the products will be considered more valuable than a $200.00 list. Such consumer behavior is that prices in an odd range are generally considered a better deal, so it is important to make sure you have chosen the right price and the right strategy for the product.

Another instance of psychological pricing is reference pricing. Reference pricing is when buyers relate psychologically to a price, as it directly reflects their relationship to the price

 THE PERFECT PRICE

of a product. In the case of high-value products, such as luxury goods, the reference price is very influential and an entire company can be capitalised on this basis.

However, care must be taken when positioning prices as the strategy can be counterproductive if the buyer feels that the product does not deserve to be in that category. If the product has the characteristics that appeal to an ego-sensitive buyer, the reference price is an appropriate pricing strategy.

An example of this is high-end luxury goods that appeal to ego-sensitive buyers. For the reference price to be successful, you must ensure that the price you have determined for a product is best adjusted from all angles and points of view, including your own.

THE PERFECT PRICE

Make sure that the price selected fits the product and that the price has been tested before it is launched into the target market. You should also consider the influence of various market elements on the price tag. The product should be suitable for a psychological pricing strategy, the promotional program should be appropriate for the pricing strategy, and the distribution channels should be synchronized with the price and not negate the cost of the product itself.

Market Penetration Prices

A fast-entry pricing strategy that assumes that sales volume increases when an object has a low price that in turn reduces overall costs is called market entry pricing. This is a useful strategy that can be used in price-sensitive markets. For example, consider the market for DVD players; this is a market where sales volumes are high, but the number of competitors is also high.

The production costs of DVD players have decreased dramatically and the constantly evolving technology has allowed the rapid introduction of new features and benefits in new models. Companies that charge for DVD players and sell large volumes at low or reasonable prices are following a strategy of market penetration.

Entrepreneurs using market penetration pricing generally try to grow a market for their brand and in the process penetrate the market for the product as a whole. All calculations are based on the assumption that the lowest price will win the most market share. But it is very important to evaluate your market, its price sensitivity and its elasticity or inelasticity before using this pricing strategy.

A certain amount of market research is also necessary so that you can understand and prejudge how your competitors will react to this penetrating pricing strategy. For example, if your low price causes your competitor to also lower the price, it will lead you to a dead end, because then you will lower your price again causing a similar reaction from him, and this will continue and no one will win.

While what was said above is true, it is also true that your market entry pricing strategy can be a deterrent to new competitors who are considering entering the market. The risk for a new entrant to gain significant market share is extremely high and when they consider how low their price is, they will see that their margin will be low and therefore consider the risks they might choose not to enter the market.

But to succeed with this strategy, you must be prepared to enjoy the economies of scale that a high volume of sales will generate and be the low-cost provider in the market. If you

THE PERFECT PRICE

have an existing business and your competitor is following a market entry strategy, you should do the same thorough research and evaluation of the market and your own capabilities:

- Is it feasible for you to reduce your costs?
- Can you be sure that you will produce large volumes?
- Can you run the risk of selling your product at a low price (and expect the sales volume to give you the market share and profitability you want)?

If you answer all of these questions in the negative, consider this penetration strategy very carefully before using it, and if you are still not sure, do not follow the strategy.

However, if you are a new business entrepreneur considering this strategy in a new or sparsely populated market where competition is low, and then focus on how to reduce your costs and increase your efficiency.

Whatever pricing strategy you decide to use, be sure to specify it in your marketing mix plan with the reasons for your choice.

Evaluate your chosen marketing strategy, including your pricing strategy at least once a year when you update your business plan, and make sure it is the right strategy for your product given the market conditions and for your consumers and competitors.

 THE PERFECT PRICE

Promotional prices

Generally, promotional prices are used when launching a new product. It is used to stimulate demand for those products that have a lagging demand. The target price buyers are usually the ones looking for the deal. Some examples of these promotional event prices are for special events. They are usually intended for certain events that could be Christmas or Easter.

There are discount or bonus programs available when buying a home. Sometimes, the seller offers a move in allowance or replacement of carpeting or renovation allowance or a refund for all cash without problems with financing or purchase of large

items such as cars. There are many stores that would not advertise interest financing loans for their purchased furniture.

The car dealer also offers these pricing programs for their previous year's models. These sales strategies have been very successful, but when using these strategies you should be careful because customers are becoming more sensitive to the true value of the strategies. Another phasing strategy that seems to work is to buy one and get one free or get two for the price of one.

This is possible if the cost of the product is low, with a healthy profit margin and also in case of inventory overload. Another important mode may be the payment mode which is the extended payment term.

THE PERFECT PRICE

You must pay a deposit and pay over a period of time. You can get the product only when you pay. This is very common in the renovation and construction industry, since payment is made first as an initial cost, then when the project is halfway through, and later on while it is being completed.

Sometimes, the guarantee of low cost or free help in these business strategies. A good product usually has no return and a customer is convinced. Therefore, these strategies have a positive impact. Overuse of these strategies has led to customer skepticism. They look for reality in the deal. The most frequently used promotional price is the "close of business" sale.

THE PERFECT PRICE

This sale can be misleading, as it can be deceptive. It is a relocation of the same business. As a customer, you should know that you are not being misled in such a scheme. There are still many effective promotional pricing programs, so be smart about how you develop your pricing strategies.

THE PERFECT PRICE

Competitive price

To determine if your items are priced too high or not, do what your customer does. Search the web.

Take any of your products and search the Internet. Compare prices with others, this will help you if you want to sell more. It's simple, you just need to write the name and ask to compare prices. It may take a little time depending on the item you sell and the market saturation. This would provide an important insight that would help your business and let you know what you're up against.

THE PERFECT PRICE

You may be able to differentiate your product and convince your customer to buy from you. Start this by reducing your cost. This always helps. If you see the possibility of lowering your prices even further, do it. You will find that your item will become the "lowest price on the web! Low cost helps you buy and this will make up for the difference in price reduction.

Guarantee a price match. Let your customers know that you will match any price and that it will not be low sold. Once the customer is there, have them continue with the purchase. You might also offer them free shipping. In case your item costs more than the competitor, you can offer free shipping as this would give your item the lowest cost at the time of payment.

THE PERFECT PRICE

Free shipping is added as a bonus to any buyer. This word makes a big difference if you finally make the sale or not. If you happen to lose a customer, it would be because the customer is not convinced by the cost of the item. Therefore, to convince your customer that your product is worth the cost and definitely worth buying, it is important that you make certain changes.

Cost is not the only factor, but one of the most important factors influencing the purchase. So, if you have given your customer a better purchase in case it is worth it, it will help them to have an advantage over the rest of the competitors.

 THE PERFECT PRICE

Offer discounts as part of your pricing strategy

The price of goods is difficult. There is no single magic formula that decides the best price for a product. There is no simple strategy, but certain steps can be taken to make pricing policies more effective. It is difficult to be sure about pricing decisions; you can only rely on your own judgment. But even while you do, the decisions are never entirely satisfactory.

The pricing of goods or services is one of the most important in business. The price of products must be set in such a way that the intended customers are willing to pay that

THE PERFECT PRICE

amount and also one that generates profit for the company or business will not last long.

There are several scientific and non-scientific approaches to pricing. The following is a framework for making pricing decisions that takes into account your costs, the effects of competition, and the customer's perception of value.

Pricing policies sometimes go unnoticed as part of marketing. They can have a substantial effect on profits, so they should be given the same consideration as promotion and advertising tactics. Variation in price can significantly change both gross margins and sales volume. This leads to indirect effects on other expenses by reducing storage costs, for example, or by creating opportunities for volume discounts with

 THE PERFECT PRICE

suppliers.

Your pricing strategy may take into account consumer discount offers that give you a commercial advantage.

You can offer cash discounts to customers who pay promptly. Therefore, this system rewards those who help the company maintain a positive and steady cash flow and reduce credit collection costs.

Quantity discounts for large orders make economic sense when the cost per unit to sell or deliver a product decreases as quantity increases. A supplier, for example, can fill an order for 12 dozen cupcakes for one customer at 10 cents each, while cupcakes on the bakery shelf can be sold to several customers

 THE PERFECT PRICE

throughout the day for 20 cents each.

This is done because there is a chance that some of the cupcakes will not be sold. Costs are also associated with keeping the store open for the convenience of random customers. There are costs associated with opening the store for the convenience of random customers.

Seasonal discounts actually reward customers who essentially help a company balance its cash flow and meet production demands.

Redemption allowances for returned old products that one can reuse or resell for profit benefit both the company and consumers.

THE PERFECT PRICE

Promotional grants often make economic sense. For example, if your product is used in advertising campaigns or promotional activities by a retail chain that also sells your product, it ends up boosting your marketing efforts. If this is the case, you may choose to discount your price to the retail chain that does so.

THE PERFECT PRICE

Alternative pricing strategies

Price is undoubtedly one of the most important factors in your marketing mix strategy. The right price can make your product a success or a failure in the marketplace. The factors to consider when marketing your product are the following:

- It has to be of superior quality.
- It must have characteristics that your buyers require or desire.
- It must be different from what your competitors have to offer.
- It must have a good cost structure.

THE PERFECT PRICE

- You must also pay attention to a strong promotional campaign.
- Taking these factors into account, it is important to determine the pricing strategy in a way that will help you successfully sell your product in the market.

Below are some alternative pricing strategies:

1. Generic or economic pricing: in this strategy, the low price attracts the buyer. This is typical of generic or economy brands. For this strategy to be successful, it must have a low cost structure, minimum features and promotion. At the same time, be sure to reap some solid and stable benefits.

2. Differential pricing: In this method, the

idea is to set the price according to different types of buyers (for example, the price will be different for an online store, a retail store, and a department store); geographic area, (prices may be higher in California than in Illinois); by quantity purchased (a person who buys large quantities will get a different rate than one who buys a small quantity); based on the national account segment (the price charged to a national account will vary from that charged to a local account). Remember, there has to be a valid reason for differential pricing.

3. Premium pricing: this strategy is applicable for luxury or high-end goods, such as expensive jewelry, yachts, airplanes, properties, etc. You can use this strategy if the market recognizes your product as a luxury or premium item

4. Pricing of captive products or complementary products: this strategy can also be adapted to the prices of the product line. In this case, the products are grouped as companions and priced accordingly. (For example, a blender and a bowl). They also consider the products as captives (e.g. a razor that can only be equipped with one particular blade). These products are often packaged in a single package. (E.g. the blades can be packed with the razor). The prices of these products outside a package generally tend to be higher.

Remember to review your products carefully before choosing a particular strategy for pricing.

Most attractive offers

The days when men swore by Gillette and women looked no further than Guerlain are gone. There are rarely monopolies in the world market, and every product in the economy has a competitor, a substitute that constantly tries to outdo the other. The most common basis for competition in these multi-product markets is price.

Generally, consumers are attracted to those items that have a lower cost of purchase than their substitute. Since there are mainly differentiated products, the overall quality is more or less the same.

THE PERFECT PRICE

Now, from the producer's point of view, the only way to reduce the price of his product is to reduce its cost. But production methods cannot be changed without changing the quality. And it goes without saying that if one has to reduce costs, quality will surely decrease as well. Another way would be to increase the scale of production. But that takes a long time. Therefore, some other measure is required for immediate effect.

Supermarkets and wholesalers use a typical method of pricing, called block pricing. When a consumer comes across a sign that says, "Milk - 1 gallon $ 3.00; 4 gallons $ 10.00", he automatically comes to a calculated observation that he is making some kind of profit by paying two dollars less if he buys it in bulk.

 THE PERFECT PRICE

Therefore, mission accomplished. Although buying products in bulk apparently reduces the cost to consumers, your spending habit would be different if you had 1 gallon of milk at your disposal instead of 4 at a time.

Another way to get the buyer's attention is to make smart offers. Everyone understands the concept of FREE. It's a short word, but it can do great things. Typically, you buy conditioners with shampoos, scrubs with soaps, and socks with shoes. So if you buy a big bottle of shampoo and get a small bottle of conditioner for FREE, that could attract a lot of buyers.

Restaurant buffets charge a fixed price per person for meals. This means that the person who eats soup, chicken Kiev and dessert pays the same as the person who eats only chicken

 THE PERFECT PRICE

and dessert. This may sound unfair to person 1, but after all, no one refused to serve him soup.

Therefore, although price is a factor, it is primarily a psychological battle where the customer is faced with many options to choose from.

THE PERFECT PRICE

Price based on value

The price of a product based on its value judgment is extremely important. Customer preferences, product benefits, company image, convenience and product quality are all subjective criteria that will help an organization understand the customer's perception of the value of its product or service.

What customers want is vital.

Are they saving money or time by buying your product? Is there a competitive advantage they gain by using your service? What are their choices? Is it convenient for

THE PERFECT PRICE

them to use your service instead of doing it themselves? What exactly does the competition demand?

The maximum price the customer will pay for the benefit received can be understood by considering the above points.

Some value-based pricing strategies are listed below. They take into account the breakeven point, but include subjective judgments in addition to numbers.

1. Same price as competitors: This is used when the prices of a commodity are generally well established (such as professional services), or when there are no other means of setting prices. The challenge, therefore, is to find out how to reduce costs to produce

higher profits compared to competitors.

2. Setting a low price: this is done only to capture a large number of customers in the market in question. This strategy is also used to achieve non-financial objectives, such as meeting the competition, projecting a low-cost image or simply getting to know the product. If profitability can be maintained at a low price, or if sales levels are acceptable, this strategy works and can then lead to higher prices.

3. Charge a high price: It is possible to charge a high price in relation to the cost of the product if it is unique and valuable to customers. The wealth of the target market also counts. Positioning a product as a "prestige product" in such a case would allow a high price to be charged. For example,

Rolex watches may not have such a high cost of production. However, the high price brings a "status" benefit to the rich Rolex market.

Charging customers what they are "willing to pay", even if it is high, is a strategy that requires alertness and intelligence. It also requires a willingness to change because customers (as well as competitors) may decide that the profits are too high. Therefore, many factors influence value-based pricing, but a smart strategist can make the most of it.

THE PERFECT PRICE

How do you know if your price is right?

If your prices aren't perfect, you won't get anywhere, even if you have the best product/service in the world. Internet companies employ three main pricing strategies: POPS, CAPS and VAPS. If implemented properly, they can help companies gain an advantage over the rest.

(POPS) PHYSICAL OBJECT PRICING STRATEGY, works well when selling a physical item and what is shipped to your customers. Amazon.com and Wall-Mart fall into this category. These companies start at the base level to determine the price by finding out how much it costs to produce and deliver an additional unit. (This is the marginal cost).

Let's take the example of Wall-Mart. They sell microwaves. To sell an additional unit, how much would it cost? To figure this out, they would have to find out the cost at which they buy from their suppliers, the cost at which they put it in the store, and the cost at which they execute their transaction. Then, to determine the final price a company needs to add to the marginal cost.

This is the operating profit margin:

To find out the percentage they need to compare it to other similar companies. Amazon has a 6% profit. Competing retailers

THE PERFECT PRICE

should aim for the same operating margin, preferably a lower one would suffice. A company that develops an efficient business process could minimize their cost and help them keep their prices low while keeping their margin attractive.

COST OF THE ACQUISITION PRICING STRATEGY. POPS works well if your primary cost is the cost of the actual cost of the goods you are delivering. But companies that sell products/services where the cost is based on marketing, associated with the number of visitors to their site, may benefit from using CAPS to determine their final price. CAPS generally answers two key questions.

1. How much will it cost to get people to visit a site?

2. What is the percentage of site visitors who would make the final purchase?

The answer to the first question should be divided by the answer to the second question to give the company its cost per acquisition. Therefore, the operating profit margin can be added to this to determine the final price.

For example, a retailer may find that, on average, it costs $0.10 for a visitor to the site and there may be 1% of visitors who make the purchase. So, from here, we simply derive the cost per acquisition. And we find out what the final price should be. The key here is to minimize the cost per acquisition.

THE PERFECT PRICE

(VAPS) VALUE-ADDED PRICING STRATEGY For companies where the marginal cost is zero, for example, in selling digital products such as e-books and online courses. VAPS works best while creating a business model where you can charge different prices to different customers.

 THE PERFECT PRICE

Visit our author page on Amazon and get more **MENTES LIBRES!**

http://amazon.com/author/menteslibres

If you wish, you can leave a comment on this book by clicking on the following link so that we can continue to grow! Thank you very much for your purchase!

https://www.amazon.com/dp/B084RN9G1B

www.ingramcontent.com/pod-product-compliance
Lightning Source LLC
Chambersburg PA
CBHW050257220526

45465CB00002B/713